Modern Industrial World

Canada

David Marshall
Margot Richardson

Wayland

MODERN INDUSTRIAL WORLD

Australia	**Portugal**
Canada	**Russia**
France	**South Africa**
Germany	**Spain**
Great Britain	**Sweden**
Japan	**The USA**

Cover: Although Canada is a vast country, most of the population lives in the modern cities in the south of the country.
Title page: Much of Canada is wilderness, covered in forest.
Contents page: The prairie region in the central Canadian provinces is ideally suited for growing grains such as wheat.

Series editor: Paul Mason
Editor: Margot Richardson
Series designer: Malcolm Walker

First published in 1995 by
Wayland (Publishers) Ltd
61 Western Road, Hove
East Sussex, BN3 1JD, England

British Library Cataloguing in Publication Data
Marshall, David
    Canada. – (Modern Industrial World Series)
    I. Title II. Richardson, Margot
    III. Series
    971.0648

ISBN 0–7502–1595–X

Typeset by Kudos Design, England
Printed and bound by G Canale & CSpA, Turin, Italy

Contents

A Vast Country

Canada's Rocky Mountains provide some spectacular scenery which attracts visitors from all over the world.

TIME ZONES

Canada has six time zones. When people in Vancouver are having their breakfast at 8.30 am, for their fellow Canadians in Newfoundland it is 2 pm, the middle of the afternoon.

Canada occupies the northern half of the North American continent. It is the second-largest country in the world after Russia, and nearly as big as the whole of Europe. It is further from east-coast Halifax to west-coast Vancouver than it is from Halifax across the Atlantic Ocean to London in Britain. With stops for sleeping and eating, it takes eight days to drive from one side to the other.

Canada is a land of extraordinary contrasts. If you travelled right across it you would pass through an enormous variety of different landscapes and communities: the high peaks of the Rocky Mountains, the rich farmland of the seemingly endless prairies and many kilometres of wilderness. There are coasts with quiet beaches, mountains that plunge directly into the sea and rivers stretching for thousands of kilometres inland. Canadians live in small towns, logging camps, mining settlements, fishing ports – and in huge modern cities.

'If you go on the Trans-Canada railway, right across the country, you see every possible type of countryside, every imaginable type of weather and meet every nationality. It is an experience everyone should have at least once in their life.' – **Sylvia O'Halloran, 36, teacher**

4

In common with other aspects of Canada, the climate is varied, ranging from hot summers to very cold winters. These extremes of temperature and the poor quality of much of the land mean that only 11 per cent of Canada's area is developed.

Canada's population lives on just 7 per cent of its land. Over 80 per cent of the people live within 300 km of the border with the USA, and most of the large cities are along this line.

The diversity in Canada extends to its people. Although the two main languages spoken are English and French, Canada is a multi-ethnic society, with people from many different cultures.

> ## CANADA AT A GLANCE
>
> Area: 9,970,610 square kilometres.
>
> Total coastline: 243,791 kilometres.
>
> Highest mountain: Mt Logan (5,951 metres) in the St Elias range (Yukon Territory).
>
> Population: 27.4 million.
>
> Main urban areas (population in millions): Toronto (3.89), Montreal (3.13), Vancouver (1.60), Ottawa/Hull (0.92).
>
> Currency: Canadian dollar, divided into 100 cents.
>
> Official languages: English and French.

Canada takes up about half of North America.

The Physical Environment

Canada has the longest coastline in the world and meets three oceans: the Pacific, the Atlantic and the Arctic. Its neighbour to the west, across the Arctic ocean, is Russia. To the north, the Canadian islands come within 800 km of the North Pole. Canada's lakes and rivers contain one-seventh of the world's fresh water, and travellers flying over parts of Canada see more water below them than land.

There are four main types of countryside. Natural forest covers almost half the country, with mixed deciduous and coniferous trees in the south-east and mainly conifers in the rest of the country. On the Arctic tundra, to the north, it is too cold for trees to grow but, in the short summer, mosses and flowers can be found. There are two main ranges of mountains: the Rockies in the west and Appalachians in the east. The prairies are a large area of treeless grassland in central Canada that stretches down into the USA.

There are many rivers and coastal inlets on Canada's west coast. Ships use them to transport timber and other products.

Canada can be divided into eight different geographic regions.

The Pacific Ranges and lowlands form Canada's westernmost region. Its islands are peaks of a mountain range that is partly covered by the Pacific Ocean. Because these mountains extend along the sea shore, British Columbia's coast has many long, narrow inlets, called fiords.

ARCTIC OCEAN
ICELAND
ARCTIC ISLANDS
Baffin Bay
ALASKA
Labrador Sea
CANADIAN SHIELD
ROCKY MOUNTAINS
PACIFIC RANGES AND LOWLANDS
Hudson Bay
NORTH PACIFIC OCEAN
INTERIOR PLAINS
HUDSON BAY LOWLANDS
CANADIAN SHIELD
APPALACHIAN REGION
ST LAWRENCE LOWLANDS
U S A
NORTH ATLANTIC OCEAN

Canada's geographic regions are each different in terms of topography, soil and vegetataion.

The snow-capped Rocky Mountains are to the east of the Pacific Ranges, and these two regions together are sometimes known as the Cordillera.

There are hundreds of Arctic islands, and almost all are within the Arctic Circle. They, and the northern mainland, have tundra landscape and only short, cool summers.

The prairies are the area of flat, fertile plains to the east of the Rockies, and include 75 per cent of Canada's farmland. There are large reserves of petroleum and natural gas in the province of Alberta in the western prairies.

The Canadian Shield is a huge, horseshoe-shaped area that takes up almost half of Canada. It is formed of hard rock covered by a thin layer of soil. Most of it is a wilderness of low hills and thousands of lakes, with hardy trees and scrub. In the north, gold, silver, zinc, uranium and copper are mined.

Surrounded by the Canadian Shield are the Hudson Bay lowlands: a flat, swampy area.

The Great Lakes form a natural barrier between the eastern parts of Canada and the USA. They are linked to the Atlantic Ocean by the St Lawrence Seaway which stretches for 4,240 km.

The St Lawrence lowlands, in the extreme south of Ontario and Québec, is the smallest region, but more than half the Canadian people live there. To the southeast is the Appalachian Highlands region, which is hilly and forested.

CLIMATE

Canada has one of the coldest climates of the developed countries of the world. Although it is extremely hot in summer in the prairies, Ontario and Québec, the January average across the country is minus 18 °C. Snow covers most of Canada from November until April.

More snow falls in Montreal than in any other city of a similar size. A huge budget is put aside for removing 40 million tonnes of snow from its streets each year.

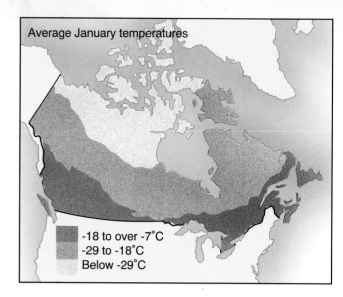

Average January temperatures

-18 to over -7°C
-29 to -18°C
Below -29°C

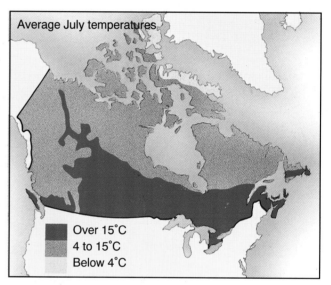

Average July temperatures

Over 15°C
4 to 15°C
Below 4°C

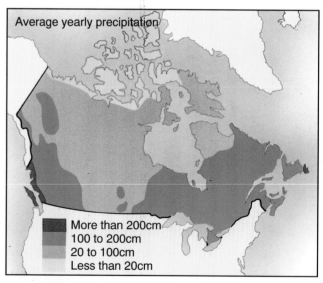

Average yearly precipitation

More than 200cm
100 to 200cm
20 to 100cm
Less than 20cm

Left *Nova Scotia's rugged coast provides many small harbours for fishing boats.*

The highest rainfall is on the west coast: over 2,500 mm a year. The prairies are fairly dry all through the year, which is one reason why cereals grow so well there.

The tides in the Bay of Fundy (between New Brunswick and Nova Scotia), are the highest in the world. The highest ever recorded was 16.6 m, the height of a four-storey building.

Snow-ploughs are an everyday sight during winter in many parts of Canada. They are used to remove snow from the roads so cars and trucks can travel about easily.

DESCRIBING THE WINDS

The Canadians give names to the winds that blow across their country. On Ellesmere Island in the Northwest Territories there is the 'cow storm' which is said to blow the horns off musk oxen. In Newfoundland they have the 'wreckhouse'. The famous 'chinook', or 'snow-eater' is a warm, south-west wind that blows off the eastern slopes of the Rockies and melts the snow to the north-west, uncovering the grass so that the animals can eat again. Some legends say that the chinook is the warm breath of a Native American princess.

WILDLIFE

Because much of the country is so undeveloped, there is a great variety of wildlife. The best known animals are moose, bears, caribou and beavers, but there are also deer, coyote, antelope, mountain lions, otters, minks, seals, walruses, owls and wolves.

Bears are part of Canadian folklore. The grizzly has a reputation for being fierce. It grows up to 275 cm tall, has thick, brown hair with white tips, and a big hump on its back behind its neck. Its amazing sense of smell makes up for its poor eyesight. It is also a very fast mover. The only way to escape from a grizzly is to climb a tree. The very common black and brown bears, however, can climb trees. They are found in remote areas all over Canada and often live close to camps and rubbish tips.

The frozen wastes of the Arctic regions are the home of the magnificent polar bear, which was hunted almost to extinction for its fur. It is now a protected animal.

The huge, solitary moose has large antlers and a thick, brown coat. It is normally a timid, shy creature, but in the autumn the male bellows for its mate and becomes aggressive towards hunters.

The grizzly bear has a fearsome reputation but attacks people only rarely. It eats everything from berries and roots to small animals.

The moose is the largest member of the deer family and stands 1.6 to 2 metres tall.

The beaver is a Canadian symbol, and the results of its industry – demolished trees and big dams of earth and wood in the middle of streams and ponds – can be seen in some wooded areas of Canada.

Hunting animals for their furs and for sport used to be common all over Canada. Now, however, many species of wild animal are protected and hunting is restricted.

Hunters used to kill wild animals for food and for their fur, but now some people enjoy hunting as a sport and recreation.

'It is hard not being able to hunt anything we want to. We have grown up with the idea that it is part of a man's life to go hunting. Many of the legends of the taming of Canada have grown up around hunting. Every year we used to pack up for a few weeks and go off to hunt. Now we have to ask permission, which is usually denied.'
– Jack Petrie, 68, a farmer in Newfoundland

The Development of Modern Canada

The first inhabitants of what is now Canada were Native American and Inuit people. It is thought that they came from Asia, more than 10,000 years ago, when Russia and Alaska were connected by land.

Vikings probably visited in about AD1000, but few Europeans knew anything about this land until the late fifteenth century. John Cabot, an Italian navigator, was employed by King Henry VII of England to find a new route to the rich trading ports of Asia. Sailing west from England, he arrived at the coast of North America. Ignoring the native people already living there, he claimed the land for England. At about the same time, sailors from Spain and Portugal may have already found the rich fishing grounds off Newfoundland's coast.

The French soon arrived as well. In 1534, Jacques Cartier was sent by King Francis I to find the fabled Northwest Passage to China. When he landed, he claimed the whole country for France.

Jacques Cartier of France was one of many explorers looking for a quick route to China and Asia.

THE START OF THE FUR TRADE

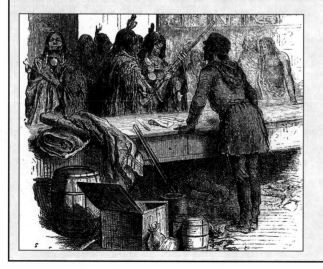

As the Canadian fishing grounds were a long way from Europe, the fishermen who went there had to preserve their catch before taking it back home to sell. They landed on the Canadian coast to dry fish in the sun, and met Native Americans who wanted to trade furs for European goods, such as knives and fish-hooks. Furs from animals such as beavers, minks and otters were not available in Europe, and could be sold for a great deal of money when the fishermen returned home.

This very early drawing – part map and part picture – shows New France and the islands off the east coast of Canada.

SETTLEMENT BY EUROPEANS

The first settlers were attracted by the valuable fur trade. In 1605, a French colony was established in what is now Nova Scotia, and others followed in the present-day provinces of Québec, New Brunswick and Prince Edward Island. The region was called New France. British settlers also came, but there was little sign of unity between the French and the British, who often fought over fur-trading and territory. There was also conflict with the Native Americans, who objected to the loss of their land.

Because of the isolation and hardships, by the 1660s there were only about 3,000 European people living in all the settlements. Even so, King Louis XIV of France made the area into an official French colony. He sent out troops to fight the Native Americans, and administrators to govern and develop the colony. The boundaries of New France started to grow more rapidly, but the British territories also expanded.

In the early 1700s, France and Britain each controlled various parts of Canada and were in dispute about others: Newfoundland and the area called Rupert's Land.

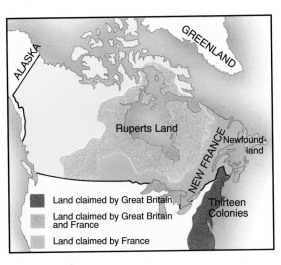

Ruperts Land

Newfoundland

NEW FRANCE

Thirteen Colonies

ALASKA

GREENLAND

- Land claimed by Great Britain
- Land claimed by Great Britain and France
- Land claimed by France

THE NAMING OF CANADA

Canada probably comes from *kanata*, an Iroquois Native American word that means village or community.

BRITISH AND FRENCH CONFLICT

The two groups of colonists fought each other in four wars between 1689 and 1760. In 1713, as a result of war between the two countries in Europe, France was forced to hand over some of its land in Canada to Britain. From then on, the French fought a losing battle for the control of Canada, and in 1763, New France became a British colony. At first, it was governed under British laws, but later, the British Parliament passed an Act allowing the French Canadians to keep their own language, laws and religion. Even so, there was often disagreement between the French- and English-speaking people in later years.

From this time, more and more British people began to arrive in Canada and they soon took over the French fur trade. Most of these furs had come from Native Americans living in the river valleys to the south. However, after the US War of Independence, these areas became part of the USA, so the traders had to find their furs elsewhere. This stimulated exploration further west, and eventually, explorers travelling from the east reached the Pacific Ocean.

Explorers used the rivers to cross the continent, but sometimes the rivers were so wild and dangerous that the explorers barely survived the journey.

IMPORTANT DATES AND EVENTS

1497	John Cabot 'discovers' Canada for Britain
1534	Jacques Cartier (French) arrives in Canada
1605	First colony established on the Bay of Fundy in present-day Nova Scotia
1663	New France officially becomes a province of France
1713	France forced to hand over much of its Canadian land to Britain
1763	Treaty of Paris signed: New France becomes a British possession
1774	British pass Act allowing French to keep their own laws and religion
1775	US War of Independence starts (ends 1781)
1793	Explorer Alexander Mackenzie reaches west coast of Canada
1812	Britain and USA at war (ends 1814)
1867	The Dominion of Canada formed and the first prime minister, John A Macdonald, elected
1931	Statute of Westminster: Canada becomes autonomous
1982	The Canada Act gives Canada complete independence

In the 1890s, the Canadian Pacific Railway was the only possible way for people to cross Canada's vast interior.

In the early 1800s there was some conflict between the British colonies in Canada and the newly independent USA to the south. The Americans declared war on the British, but once the war was resolved, the population began to grow rapidly as thousands of migrants arrived from Britain and Ireland.

As the various colonies grew, their people pushed for Canadian self-government. Gradually, the colonies joined together into the Dominion of Canada.

British Columbia agreed to join the confederation only if a railway line was built linking one coast to the other. The Canadian Pacific line was finished in 1885, opening up the huge area between Manitoba and British Columbia. A publicity campaign was started, promising a free farm to people who could establish themselves there, and new immigrants were attracted from all over Europe and Canada.

15

TWENTIETH-CENTURY DEVELOPMENTS

Canada played an important role in the First World War, and so was granted representation on the League of Nations in its own right, rather than as part of Britain. From the 1930s, Canada was able to start playing its own part in international affairs, including being a founder member of the United Nations and NATO.

A 1914 advertisement encouraging people to emigrate to Canada. It promised health, wealth and free land.

In the 1960s there were two further important breaks in Canada's ties with Britain. Canada ceased to use the British national anthem and flag, replacing the anthem with 'O Canada', and adopting the Maple Leaf flag.

The Canada Act, passed in 1982, gave Canada its complete independence, although it is still a member of the British Commonwealth.

THE ACADIANS

When the French first settled around the Bay of Fundy in 1605, they called the area Acadia. After living there for about a hundred years, they had begun to call themselves Acadians. When the French were forced to hand the area over to the British, the Acadians refused to take an oath of allegiance to their new rulers

For a time they were left alone, but when a new governor, Charles Lawrence, was appointed in 1754 he insisted that they agreed to swear an oath of allegiance to Britain. The Acadians refused. In August 1755 Lawrence ordered expulsions to begin and 14,000 Acadians were forced out of the area. Their houses and villages were burnt. Many of the people settled in Louisiana and New Orleans in the USA where their name became Cajun. The Cajuns have managed to preserve their culture even today.

Most of the French-speaking people now living in Nova Scotia, Prince Edward Island and New Brunswick are descendants of the original Acadians. They have their own festivals, fly their own flag and play their own distinctive music.

LAND CLAIM AGREEMENTS

Recently, the Canadian government has reconsidered the position of its original native peoples. The attitude towards the rights of these groups to their land has gradually mellowed. In 1975, the first land claim agreement to properly address people's concerns about land ownership was made with the Cree Native Americans and the Inuit living in the James Bay area.

In 1993, the decision was made to divide the current Northwest Territories into two, creating the Nunavut Territory, in which the Inuit will be able to have a form of self-government. *Nunavut* means 'our land', and is a recognition that the Inuit are a part of Canada's future, not a symbol of its past.

Inuit people wearing traditional fur clothing to protect them from the intense cold of their native environment.

Agriculture and Fishing

Agriculture is less important to Canada now than it was in the country's early years, but a wide range of produce is still grown. Agricultural output makes up 3 per cent of the country's Gross Domestic Product (the wealth a country makes within its borders) and farm workers number about 4 per cent of the population.

There are four distinct farming regions. Most farmers carry out mixed farming, as some crops can be grown alongside livestock, such is the richness of Canadian land.

In the Atlantic area, some of the best potatoes in North America are grown.

In the St Lawrence lowlands, which include both the damp, fertile soil near the St Lawrence Seaway and the sunny climate of southern Québec and Ontario, cereals, vegetables and fruit, such as grapes, peaches and tomatoes, are produced. This area is also ideal for rearing beef and dairy cattle. Most of the country's famous maple syrup is produced here, too.

Many types of vegetables are grown in the fertile south east.

Only the south of Canada is mild enough for crops.

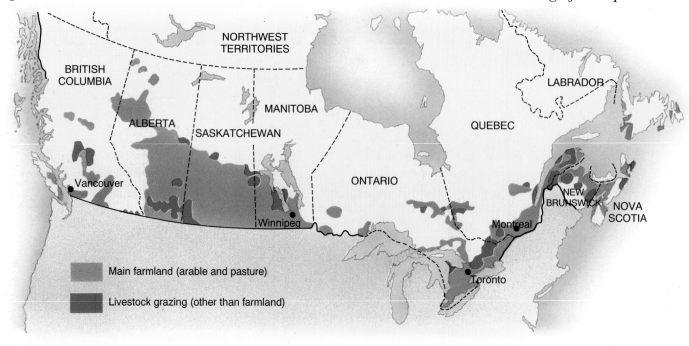

NORTHWEST TERRITORIES

BRITISH COLUMBIA

LABRADOR

ALBERTA

MANITOBA

SASKATCHEWAN

QUEBEC

Vancouver

ONTARIO

Winnipeg

NEW BRUNSWICK

NOVA SCOTIA

Montreal

Toronto

Main farmland (arable and pasture)

Livestock grazing (other than farmland)

In terms of exports, wheat, grown throughout the prairies, is the most important crop. In the past, the climate in the prairies made the land difficult to manage. Dust storms regularly blew away the layer of fertile top soil. It is one of Canada's success stories that, in the course of the last fifty years, technological developments in farming have made this regions very profitable, with annual wheat crops of over 25 million tonnes. The prairies are also home to some very large herds of both beef and dairy cattle.

The farming land on the British Columbia side of the Rockies, bathed in a warm climate, yields bumper harvests of fruit – especially apples, for which Canada is famous – and vegetables. As in other regions, farmers here raise both cash crops and dairy cattle.

Maple syrup is made from the sap of maple trees. The sap is collected in a bucket from a cut in the tree trunk, then boiled down to form a sweet, runny syrup.

MAIN FARM PRODUCTS	
	Value, 1992 $ (thousands)
Wheat	2,625,302
Oats and barley	549,773
Canola	968,414
Potatoes	362,415
Vegetables	767,983
Fruit	393,067
Tobacco	330,517
Cattle and calves	4,579,959
Pigs	1,758,759
Sheep and lambs	43,302
Dairy products	3,043,520
Poultry and eggs	1,645,414

Statesman's Yearbook, 1994–95

Agricultural machinery and equipment also owes a great deal to Canadian inventors. For example, in recent years, the flexible combine header, which adjusts itself to uneven land, has been developed.

Canada's enormous wheat crops, grown on the prairies, need huge storage buildings. Canada's unique grain stores are the country's most distinctive form of architecture. Known as 'the castles of the New World' they are big buildings, about 10 metres square by 20 metres high.

Wheat and other grains that have been harvested are stored in the distinctive silos that dot the prairie landscape.

FISHING

Fishing is Canada's oldest industry, and fishing communities still thrive on both the east and west coasts. In fact, Canada is the world's biggest exporter of fish.

On the Pacific coast the main catch is salmon. Fishing trawlers work out of many ports along the coast of British Columbia, because each year the salmon flock to the rivers along the coastline to spawn.

Trawlers off British Columbia use long nets for catching salmon.

The Grand Banks, off the coast of Newfoundland, is one of the world's richest fishing grounds. Cod fishing has been established for hundreds of years, and lobsters, crabs and scallops are other important money earners.

Pollution of all marine life has threatened the continued success of this industry, and over-fishing has led to the reduction in both the amount of time fishermen are permitted to spend on the water in any one session, and in the amount they will catch. However, the traditional fishing skill of 'watching the water' – of getting to know the sea so well that you know where fish are most likely to be – continues to be passed down the generations. This skill enables the fishermen to bring in the catches, for the time being at least.

Fishing has been an important industry off Canada's east coast for more than 500 years, but many local people are afraid that over-fishing could damage their livelihood.

Trade and Industry

JOBS THAT CANADIANS DO	
	Number of workers
Agriculture, hunting, forestry, fishing	533,000
Mining and quarrying	157,000
Manufacturing	1,788,000
Electricity, gas and water	149,000
Construction	681,000
Trade, restaurants and hotels	2,917,000
Transport and communications	773,000
Finance, insurance, real estate and business services	1,439,000

ILO Year Book of Labour Statistics, 1992 figures

Canada is the seventh-largest trading nation in the world. It is a member of the Group of Seven most industrialised nations, known as the G7 countries. The other members are the USA, Japan, Germany, France, the UK and Italy.

Canada became wealthy because it has vast reserves of natural resources. Furs were the first valuable export. Later it was found that Canada has enormous deposits of minerals, including zinc, nickel, gold, silver, iron ore, uranium, copper, cobalt and lead. As well, there are large stocks of crude oil and natural gas. Water is also used to generate huge amounts of hydro-electricity.

One of the things that has made Canada wealthy is its huge deposits of minerals. This mine and mill produce uranium for nuclear power. Canada is the world's leading exporter of uranium .

Hydro-electric power supplies over 60 per cent of the country's needs for electricity. The remainder is produced from coal and nuclear power. Exporting hydro-electrical energy to the USA has become increasingly important.

The main manufacturing industries are heavy industries. They produce iron and steel for the motor industry, as well as making motor vehicles, industrial and agricultural machinery. Other industries include textile, timber and paper production, and food processing.

Industrial areas are concentrated mainly in southern Ontario (52.8 per cent of the national total) and Québec (24.7 per cent). Here they are close the USA, and to shipping on the Great Lakes and the St Lawrence Seaway.

Today, however, service industries employ more people than any other type of industry. These include transportation, banking and insurance.

A forestry worker, or lumberjack, fells a mature tree. Although Canada has vast areas of forest, replanting trees is also important to ensure supplies for the future.

THE TIMBER AND PAPER INDUSTRY

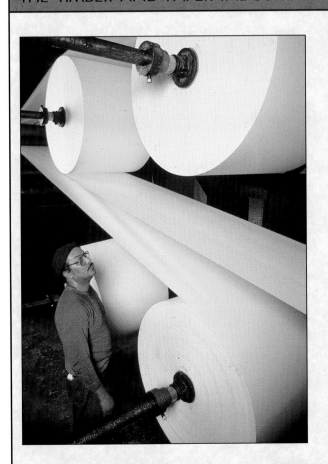

About 40 per cent of Canada's land is covered by forest, and forest-based industries make a big contribution to its economy. Some of the wood is used for timber, but the most important products are wood pulp and paper, especially newsprint. Canada supplies nearly a third of all the newsprint paper used throughout the world.

In 1993, Canadian paper and allied products were worth $US22 billion.

Newsprint paper is one of Canada's major export products.

Three-quarters of Canada's trade is with the USA, creating the world's largest trade route that operates between just two countries. In fact, the USA dominates the Canadian economy, and many US companies have set up in Canada to avoid US taxes.

The two nations operate under a special agreement that avoids taxes on imports and exports: the North American Free Trade Agreement, signed in 1992 by the leaders of Canada, USA and Mexico.

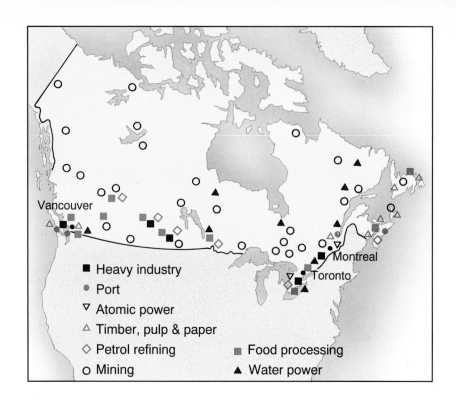

- ■ Heavy industry
- ● Port
- ▽ Atomic power
- △ Timber, pulp & paper
- ◇ Petrol refining
- ○ Mining
- ■ Food processing
- ▲ Water power

Manufacturing in Canada is mainly found in the south, close to markets in the USA and transport by ship to the rest of the world.

IMPORTS AND EXPORTS, 1993	
	Percentage
Exports	
Automotive products	24.5
Industrial goods and materials	22.5
Machinery and equipment	17.6
Forestry products	15.9
Energy products	8.7
Agriculture and Fishing	8.3
Other	2.5
Imports	
Machinery and equipment	32.2
Automotive products	23.8
Industrial goods and materials	19.7
Other consumer goods	11.2
Agriculture and fishing	6.1
Energy	4.6
Forestry	1.0
Other	1.4

Canada Study Pack, Commonwealth Institute

An engineering success story

Bombardier, one of Canada's leading manufacturing companies, started in a garage in the village of Valcourt in Québec. Joseph-Armand Bombardier, born in 1907, was fascinated by machinery and wanted to design vehicles to travel on Canada's snow-covered roads. At the age of nineteen, he set himself up as a mechanic, devoting all his spare time to his own research.

By 1936, Bombardier had invented and patented a 'snowmobile' to carry seven people. The vehicle became very popular. In 1940, Bombardier started his first factory with a small group of workers he had trained himself. During the Second World War, the Bombardier company improved its design and supplied the army with an armoured snowmobile known as the Kaki.

The real breakthrough came with Bombardier's most famous vehicle, the 'skidoo', in 1959. The tracks were superior to those on earlier snowmobiles and the engines were lighter. Winter sports enthusiasts around the world applauded the skidoo and 225 sales were made in the first winter alone.

Following the death of Joseph-Armand, in 1964, Bombardier has remained the leader of the competitive snowmobile market in Canada, North America and parts of Europe. It has also diversified into off-road motorcycles, boats and railway rolling stock.

The skidoo can skim quickly over thick snow. It is the major form of transport in some country areas, but some people ride just for fun.

TOURISM

Canada makes part of its wealth from the large number of tourists who visit the country each year. They come to see the magnificent scenery, to explore the wilderness areas, see the wildlife, and experience the attractions of its cities. There are many outdoor activities to be enjoyed, such as hiking, camping, canoeing and skiing. The cities provide a variety of entertainment, and restaurants serving food from all over the world as a result of Canada's multi-ethnic population. The most popular destinations are British Columbia and the Rockies, Toronto, Montreal and Niagara Falls.

Tourists bring money to spend on accommodation, eating and drinking, and to buy goods and souvenirs. This extra money brought into the country provides employment for the many Canadians who work in hotels, restaurants and shops.

NUMBER OF TOURISTS	
From USA	32,427,000
From other countries	3,303,000

Europa World Yearbook, 1994
(1992 figures)

The tourist industry attracts money into Canada and provides employment for many of its people.

26

These two women are working on a fish stall at Steveston fish market in Vancouver. Their stall is right beside the mooring for the boats.

The construction industry employs more people than agriculture, forestry and fishing put together.

A GROWING ECONOMY

Since the beginning of the 1980s, Canada's economic growth has been remarkable. Between 1984 and 1988, its Gross Domestic Product grew at a rate of 4.7 per cent per year. As well, in the 1980s Canada had the fastest growing labour force of any of the G7 countries. The growth in the number of working people was about 2 per cent per year, probably due to the large numbers of people who emigrated to Canada.

However, in recent years, both the number of part-time jobs and unemployment have risen. In 1993 the unemployment rate was 11.8 per cent, and it is increasing.

Canada's labour laws do not allow discrimination in employment. This has led to a big change in women's lives. Women make up over half the Canadian labour force, but most women take up only low-paid or part-time work so, on average, they earn only two-thirds of the salary of men.

Huge trains – often more than 1 km long – transport freight across the country.

The St Lawrence Seaway links the Great Lakes with the Atlantic Ocean, and is controlled jointly by Canada and the USA.

TRANSPORT

Because it is such a vast country, Canada needs efficient communications of all kinds.

The Trans-Canada Highway, completed in 1962, is the longest one-nation highway in the world. It is more than 7,699 km long and runs through all ten provinces, from Newfoundland in the east to Victoria in British Columbia.

In the winter, some lakes and rivers freeze to a depth of a metre and enable cars, coaches and trucks to travel further north than they can in the summer months.

Rail links right across the country were first established in 1885 with the completion of the Canadian Pacific Railway. This railway and The Canadian National Railway network are still the most important carriers of freight across the country.

The huge length of coastline, including 3,000 km of inland waterways, means that shipping has always been an important form of transport in Canada. There are 25 large deep-water ports and about 650 smaller ports. Some of the deep-water ports are on the St Lawrence Seaway, the world's longest canal system. Ice-breakers keep the seaway open for most of the year.

Canadian aeroplane manufacturers are pioneers in short take-off and landing aircraft, such as the Canadair. They have also developed a special fire-fighting plane that can scoop up over 6 tonnes of water from a lake or the sea and drop it on a forest fire with amazing accuracy. These aircaft are now in use all over the world.

Seaplanes are often used in remote areas. There is almost always somewhere for them to land.

MODERN COMMUNICATIONS

Living in a wealthy, industrial nation, Canadians have the use of every type of modern communications, including computers, telephones, faxes and modems. Television and radio broadcast in both English and French, and there are some radio programmes in Native American and Inuit languages. Satellite television is beamed to remote locations, and three-quarters of Canadian homes subscribe to cable television.

Some people in remote areas are able to communicate using small, portable dishes linked up to a mobile communications satellite. Satellites also provide information on natural resources to the Canadian Centre for Remote Sensing.

About 100 daily newspapers are printed in English, 10 in French, and about 75 newspapers in a variety of other languages. There are more than 1,350 magazines published, plus about 4,000 new books per year.

Computer-based learning is common in schools, and in some remote areas, it helps to overcome the disadvantages of distance from other communities.

'There are children in Canada who know more about China and Brazil than they do about Québec or the Yukon; all because of the invention of the telephone and the modem. Of course, modern technology shrinks the world and makes everywhere accessible. I wonder if it will make Canadians tolerate each other any better?'
– Susan Bridges, a teacher in Vancouver

The IMAX Corporation

IMAX is a Canadian company that creates the largest cinema screens and films in the world, with huge 'wrap-around' screens for specially developed films. The technology uses the largest possible motion-picture system, with six-channel multi-way sound, to make audience feel that they are taking part in the film. As IMAX says: 'You don't just watch a film, you feel you are in it.'

The company has made many special films that allow this effect to be exploited, such as *The Secret of Life on Earth, Into the Deep* and *Mountain Gorilla*.

A Canadian zoologist, Craig Sholley, said: 'Trying to realistically describe the true sensations of being in a forest with a family of gorillas is impossible. *Mountain Gorilla*, however, accomplishes . . . what I've never been able to adequately describe in words. It's the next best thing to being there.'

One of IMAX's newest films gives a vivid 'you are there' view of space exploration.

A Multicultural Society

Canada is a multicultural society. In fact, the world multicultural originated in Canada, to describe the way that so many different ethnic groups have come together. In the 1970s and 1980s large numbers of people from all over the world came to live in Canada. In the 1980s alone, more than a million immigrants came from more than a hundred countries.

However, most Canadians (about 73 per cent) can trace their origins to the British Isles or to France.

Because both English and French are spoken in Québec, signs can sometimes be confusing.

FRENCH-SPEAKING CANADA

It was the seventeenth-century French explorer Samuel de Champlain who gave the name Kebek to an area of Canada, and it has been French ever since. When the Dominion of Canada was created in 1867, almost a million of the inhabitants, a third of the country's total, were French speaking. It is still a shock to visitors today to find just how French Québec really is. It is the largest of Canada's provinces, and today about 80 per cent of its population speaks French as a first language, and almost 90 per cent are Roman Catholic. It is not surprising that Québec has a strong independence movement.

Montreal is sometimes called 'the Paris of North America' and is the second-largest French-speaking city in the world; only Paris itself is bigger. Almost everyone on the street, in cafés, in commerce and industry speaks French, and most Québec school children are taught in French only. The are some English speakers as well but, French is the official language in government and business.

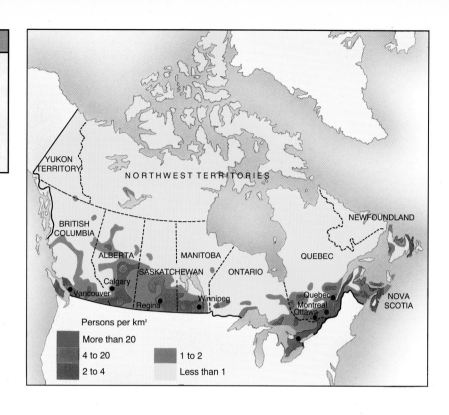

POPULATION
Of the total population of 27 million in 1991, 22.3 million were Canadian born and 4.7 million were foreign born.

The road system in the city can be confusing as the street names are written in French, but sometimes have English names as well. For example, one of the main streets in the centre of the city is called The Main by the English speakers, but it is officially called Boulevard Saint Laurent. The high ground that forms the city's biggest park is called 'the mountain' by some. It is officially known as Mont Royal, hence Montreal.

Above *The majority of Canadian people live in the southern quarter of the country.*

EDUCATION

Each province is responsible for its own school system, but all Canadian children start Grade 1 in the September before their sixth birthday, and must stay in school until they are sixteen. About 90 per cent of schools are run by the government.

English is spoken in most lessons, except in Québec. Many areas throughout Canada have introduced the French Immersion programme. This scheme means that all subjects of the curriculum are taught in French. Children there are introduced to this programme right from Grade 1.

Right *Students who cannot walk to school travel on distinctive yellow buses.*

OTHER CULTURAL INFLUENCES

There are about one and a half million Canadians of German origin. The first came in the seventeenth and eighteenth centuries, and after the First World War the poverty, deprivation and political upheavals in Europe convinced many more to emigrate and start a new life.

German Canadians have retained many of their traditional festivals and the Oktoberfest is one of the biggest events in the region. It takes place in Ontario and lasts for nine days, attracting over 500,000 visitors who enjoy the beer halls, dancing and German music.

After 1896, the Canadian government encouraged Ukrainians, Czechs, Slovaks, Poles, Hungarians, Serbs and Croats to come to Canada to settle in the prairies. Another 34,000 Ukrainians came after the Second World War. In 1990, a Ukrainian Canadian, Ray Hnatyshyn, was sworn in as Canada's governor general.

PLACE OF BIRTH OF IMMIGRANTS	
	Percentage of total (approx)
Africa	3.8
Asia	24.5
Caribbean	5.3
Europe	37.9
South and Central America	5.0
United Kingdom	16.5
USA	5.7
Other	1.3
Canada Business Facts, 1994 (Figures for 1991)	

Ukrainian Canadians at a festival in Toronto. They are wearing Ukrainian national dress.

Asians, especially Chinese, first came to Canada in 1858 to work in the gold fields on the west coast. Later they worked in dreadful conditions on the construction of the Canadian Pacific Railway. At first the Chinese were not trusted by other Canadians. They were not allowed to buy land and had to pay a head tax. For this reason, many Chinese men came to Canada alone and sent money back to their families in China. Immigration restrictions on Asians were lifted in 1967, so the Chinese population is now about 450,000.

Between 1975 and 1980, about 60,000 refugees came from Cambodia, Laos and Vietnam.

Many Canadian cities have their own 'Chinatown' where Asian people go to meet and shop.

MAIN RELIGIONS	
	Percentage of population
Roman Catholic	46.2
United Church of Canada	17.5
Anglican	11.8
Other	24.5
World Travel Guide, 1994	

35

There were two huge waves of immigration from Italy: from 1900 to 1914 and from 1950 to 1970. Italians now make up 10 per cent of the inhabitants of Toronto. Like most new immigrants, the Italians like to keep their own culture, and often a 'Little Italy' develops in large cities or towns.

'In my country the life expectancy for a woman is 45 years. In Canada it is 81 years for a woman and 71 years for a man. Can you think of a better reason for coming here?'
– Minh Luong , 31, an immigrant from Vietnam

THE MENNONITES

The Mennonites are a strict religious people who originally came from northern Europe and settled in southern Manitoba and southern Ontario in the early 1800s.

Mennonites are easy to recognize in their plain, old-fashioned clothes. They refuse to adopt modern ways, using horse-drawn carriages for transport, living on their farm produce and by selling hand-made goods. Most Mennonite homes are very basic with no electricity, radio, TV or telephone.

The Amish, a branch of the Mennonites, are even stricter in their beliefs. They do not wear buttons on their clothes as they believe they are unnecessary ornaments.

Old-fashioned Amish horse-drawn buggies display traffic reflectors to comply with modern road rules.

36

An immigrant's story

Jane Kay is an immigrant who has lived in and around Toronto for twenty-five years. She emigrated in 1970 when she was just 20 years old.

She lives in Kitchener, Ontario, 80 km from Toronto, and is an accountant in a trucking company that specializes in transporting air freight to and from Pearson International Airport. The company is quite small, just 21 employees, but successful. It was started by an Irish immigrant in 1956.

Jane believes that Canada is a land of opportunity and enterprise. 'As an immigrant, you are given the opportunity to start a new life. All you have to do is take advantage of the resources that will help you to succeed.' She was able to pick up her education, which has led her to get a good job, and she was quickly able to buy her own home.

People from the Caribbean islands participate in a Toronto festival.

Méti people are proud of their unique heritage, which can be traced back to both French and Native American ancestors.

THE FIRST NATIONS

The Canadian constitution recognizes three categories of First Nations: that is, the nations of people already living in Canada before European settlement. Together, they make up just 1.5 per cent of the total population, but they form separate groups in the Assembly of First Nations, the native council of Canada.

The Métis, (pronounced may-tee), are people of mixed Native American and French blood. Many Métis can trace their families back to original French settlers. In the years following the original French settlement the numbers of Métis grew and many settled in the Winnipeg area. They began to see themselves as a separate people with a distinct culture and defended their claim to independence in uprisings of 1869 and 1885. As a result, the province of Manitoba was created for them.

In 1983 the Métis National Council was formed, and a Métis, the Honourable Yvon Dumont, was appointed Lieutenant Governor of Manitoba in 1993.

The Native Americans are the largest group of First Nations and are split into several cultures: Eastern Woodland Indians, Plains Indians, Plateau Indians, Northwest Coast Indians and Sub-Arctic Indians. There are 595 native groups, many of which have different traditions and languages.

The Inuit used to be known as Eskimos. (Eskimo means 'raw meat eater'; Inuit means 'the people'.) They have always lived in the tundra and Arctic areas, hunting fish, seal and walrus, and trading in fur. For many centuries the Inuit lived in complete isolation and it was only the whaling trade, which began during the nineteenth century, that brought continued contact with Europeans.

Today, most Inuit live in centrally heated homes with electricity and hot water at the touch of a button. They largely manage their own affairs, and have their own area councils. There are runways for aircraft in many of their remote areas.

Two Inuit girls on a bicycle in Nain, Labrador. The right of Native American and Inuit people to control their affairs and manage their own communities is slowly being recognized by the Canadian government.

39

Government and Politics

Canada is a federation made up of ten provinces and two territories. The head of state is the British Queen Elizabeth II. She is represented in Canada by a governor general and in each province by a lieutenant governor. The Canada Act of 1982 gave Canada total control over its constitution, and severed the legal ties between itself and the United Kingdom.

Canada's method of government is based on the British system. There is a federal parliament made up of two houses: the House of Commons and the Senate, with the prime minister as leader. The House of Commons has 295 members and the Senate has a maximum of 112. Elections for members of the Commons must be held at least every five years. The Senate's members are appointed by the governor general, on the advice of the prime minister, to represent the provinces.

The main political parties are the Liberal Party (currently in power), the Bloc Québécois (the official opposition), the New Democratic Party, the Reform Party and the Progressive Conservatives.

Each of the provinces has its own parliament, which controls areas such as education, health service and the use of natural resources. The queen is represented in each province by a lieutenant governor. The Yukon and Northwest Territories are governed directly by Ottawa, but are becoming increasingly independent.

A demonstration by supporters of independence in Québec. Their signs read 'Next year my country'.

NATIONAL UNITY

There has always been some conflict between French- and English-speaking people. One of the main threats to Canada's unity is the desire for independence by the French-speaking province of Québec. The 1970s brought a major movement to make French Québec a separate state. In 1976, the separatist Parti Québécois came to power in Québec's provincial elections. It vowed to make Québec independent, but voters rejected this in 1980. However, in September 1994, the Parti Québécois was again victorious, and there is renewed pressure for independence.

WOMEN IN POLITICS

Women were given the vote in Canada in 1916. Agnes McPhail was Canada's first woman MP. She was elected in 1921 and fought for the next nineteen years to achieve equal status for women. She led the famous legal battle to alter the British North American Act, which had ruled that women were not 'persons' and were not, therefore, eligible to be appointed to the Senate.

In 1988, there were 40 women among the 295 members elected to parliament. One of them was Kim Campbell, who became Canada's first ever female prime minister, from June to October, 1993.

The Mounted Police are well known for their colourful uniforms, but also have an important role in enforcing federal laws across the country.

ROYAL CANADIAN MOUNTED POLICE

The 'Mounties', as they are popularly known, were first formed in 1873. They not only keep law and order, but also make sure that federal laws are observed. These days there are about 20,000 in the force, who operate all over the country, especially in the more sparsely populated areas. The bigger provinces and towns also have their own, separate police forces.

Sport

In Canada, children are taught to skate from a very early age, and there are many ice rinks, particularly in winter, when new rinks are easily created in parks and back yards. Speed and figure skating are also very popular. In 1984, Gaetan Boucher won two gold medals and a bronze at the Olympics for speed skating.

People pack into stadiums to watch the national game, ice hockey, which began in Montreal in 1875. Canada is very proud to have created its own sport. The National Hockey League includes seven Canadian teams. The Canada Cup draws teams from places as far away as Russia and Scandinavia, and many supporters come to see how the world as a whole plays this Canadian game.

Several Canadian sports owe their origins to the country's native people. Lacrosse's reputation as a sport for the tough comes from the fact that it was originally used by the Iroquois Indians in the training of their warriors. The kayak is a one-person canoe and was originally used by the Inuit people as a hunting vessel, but is now used mainly in sport. The word toboggan is found in the Alongquin and the Micmac languages, and meant a piece of wood that was turned up at one end. For centuries, before the existence of any snowmobiles, toboggans were used to enable people to get around in many snow-covered areas.

Ice hockey is a fast-moving game, and players wear protective clothing in case they are hit by the sticks or other players.

Cowboys and rodeos are important features of Canadian culture. The Calgary Stampede is heralded as 'The Greatest Outdoor Show on Earth' and includes events such as saddle bronc riding, steer wrestling and calf roping. Horses are specially trained to be able to cope with the demands of this world-famous event, and cowboys from across North America are always keen to take part.

Skiing is also very popular and ski resorts such as Whistler, in British Columbia, attract many visitors each year. There are also many demanding cross country routes. Olympic skiing success has also been achieved by Canadian skiers, including Karen Percy, who has led an upsurge in women's skiing.

In the summer, baseball and water sports are most popular. Baseball fans particularly remember October 1992, when the Toronto Blue Jays became the first team from outside the USA to win the famous World Series.

'It was very moving to watch groups of friends and relatives sitting together during the opening ceremony (of the Commonwealth Games held in Canada in 1994), waving their flags. I saw one grandmother proudly waving a Scottish flag, while her teenage granddaughter was just as proudly waving the Canadian Maple Leaf.'
– Newspaper journalist, August 1994

Facing the Future

Ever since the first people began to settle in Canada, it has been seen as a land where a new and better life could be made. Immigrants from all over the world still flock to Canada for the chance to join in the country's growth and prosperity. They are attracted by the vast open spaces, the industry and trading opportunities, the true democracy and equal opportunities that are offered.

In order to protect all its citizens, especially those new to the country, Canada decided, in 1982, to publish a Charter of Rights and Freedoms. The Charter included

- freedom to meet and discuss politics
- freedom of thought, conscience and religion
- freedom of the press
- the right to vote freely
- the right to live and move where you want to
- the right to a fair trial and legal help
- the right to speak your own language
- equal opportunities.

With these safeguards and opportunities it is not surprising that so many people still flock to live in Canada.

Canada's breath-taking scenery and wide open spaces are a major attraction for visitors from elsewhere, as well as being appreciated by people living in Canada.

44

However, despite the best efforts of its government, Canada still has problems to solve. The worldwide recession has hit Canada hard. Unemployment is still rising. The native people still believe they have lost their land, and although they have received some compensation, their resentment continues to grow.

French- and English-speaking Canadians are still unable to agree on a form of government that will enable them to stay together as one, united country. Although the Canadian prime minister, Jean Chretien, said, 'I am convinced that in the coming months the Québecers will again demonstrate their profound attachment to being a full part of Canada', the recent voting in Québec seems to show something else. Canada will continue to struggle to keep the country united for many years to come.

Although Canada is largely a wealthy country, it must continue to look after its ethnic minorities if everyone is to have equal opportunities and a reasonable standard of living.

45

Glossary

Arctic Any land falling within the Arctic circle, close to the North Pole.

Cereal A grain, such as wheat, oats and barley, grown for people or animals to eat.

Colonist A settler or person living in a colony.

Colony A settlement in a new country, usually controlled by a mother country elsewhere.

Confederation A group of people, areas or countries, usually having similar ideas and aims.

Conifer A cone-bearing tree, such as a pine tree.

Deciduous A type of tree that loses its leaves in autumn and grows new ones the following spring.

Emigrate To leave one country and settle in another.

Export To sell, or send out goods to another country.

Folklore Traditional beliefs, stories, music or art.

Gross Domestic Product The wealth a country produces within its borders. Also called GDP.

Immigrant A person who has arrived in a new country to live.

Independent Not depending or relying on any other country, state or person.

Labour force The number of people who are able to work in a country.

multicultural People or things from many different cultures or countries.

Prairies The name for a large area of fertile, treeless grassland in central Canada and USA.

Recession A time of economic weakness marked by a fall in the value of money, and often an increase in unemployment.

Separatism The wish of some people from part of a country to be separate and independent from the rest of the country.

Social security Financial help from the government for people who are ill, old or have lost their jobs.

Spawn Egg-laying by fish, such as salmon.

Tundra A vast, level, treeless Arctic region with hardly any soil.

Urban Built-up areas where many people live.

Further Information

Canada Study Pack, Commonwealth Institute, Kensington High Street, London W8 6NQ

BOOKS
Non-fiction

The Arctic by Sue Bullen (Wayland, 1993)
Our Country: Canada by Susan Williams (Wayland, 1990)
The Prairies and Their People by David Flint (Wayland, 1993)
Threatened Cultures: Inuit by Bryan and Cherry Alexander (Wayland, 1992)
Threatened Cultures: Native Americans by James Wilson (Wayland, 1992)
The World's Rivers: The St Lawrence by Julia Waterlow (Wayland, 1994)

Fiction

Anne of Green Gables (and other books in the same series) by L M Montgomery, (Puffin, 1994). Classic stories that have been best-sellers for over fifty years.
Paradise Cafe and Other Stories by Martha Brooks (Scholastic, 1993). Stories about teenagers, living in the prairie region.
Honor Bound by Mary Alice and John Downie (Quarry Press, 1993). The adventure story of a family at the time of the American Revolution.
Legends of Vancouver by E Pauline Johnson-Tekahionwake (Quarry Press, 1991)
Underground to Canada by Barbara Smucker (Heinemann Education, 1986). Based on a true story of two Negro slave girls making a dangerous journey to freedom in Canada.

For more advanced readers

The Salterton Trilogy by Robertson Davies (Penguin, 1992)
Murther and Walking Spirits by Robertson Davies (Penguin, 1992)
Solomon Gursky Was Here by Mordecai Richler (Vintage, 1991)

FILMS

A variety of short geography films and history videos about Canada are available from International Telefilm Enterprises Ltd, London. Tel 0171 491 1441.

PICTURE ACKNOWLEDGEMENTS
Grateful thanks for the following for allowing their photographs to be reproduced in this book:
Action-Plus 42 (G Kirk); Bryan and Cherry Alexander 17; Bombadier Engineering 25; Camera Press contents page (G Hunter), 22, 43 (T Hanley); Eye Ubiquitous 10 bottom (L Fordyce), 18 (L Fordyce), 19 (Trip/W Fraser), 21 (L Fordyce), 28 top (J Winder), 28 bottom (L Fordyce); IMAX® Corporation 31; Impact Photos Ltd title page (H Hughes/Visa), 20 bottom (A Binder), 27 top (M Dent), 29 (A Binder), 33 (A le Garsmeur), 45 (A le Garsmeur); Peter Newark's Historical Pictures 12 top and bottom, 14, 15, 16; Rex Features 40; Topham Picture Source 4, 34 (E Jones), 36 (E Jones), 39 (Eastcott/The Image Works), 41, 44; Zefa Picture Library (UK) Ltd 6, 8, 9, 10 top (D Gulin),20 top 23 top, 23 bottom (J T Miller), 26, 27 bottom, 30, 35, 36, 38 (R Bond).
All other photographs supplied by the Wayland Picture Library.
Maps were provided by Peter Bull.

Index

The figures in **bold** refer to photographs and maps.